Black Excellence Affirmations for Kids

Positive Affirmations for Black Kids to Increase Confidence, Motivation, Self-Esteem, Leadership, and Fun!

Tasha Tinsley

Contents

Introduction

My name is Tasha, and my mission in life is to empower everyone around me, and (starting today) that includes YOU!

As black people, we know we have a lot of challenges.

And being a kid... HOLY COW, it's hard. But I totally get it. And I here to help.

I don't want to turn this into a science lesson, but tons of research has taught us that when you surround yourself with positive thoughts... they positively affect you. And I know how easy it can be to be negative. That ends today!

When you read, listen to, and repeat positive thoughts (I call them affirmations), your mind and body experience joy, wonder, fulfillment, and happiness. And we all need more of that!

Treat this book like a firehose of positivity. Surround yourself with it. Drink it up. It will make you the best version of yourself.

You can use this book a little bit every day or just when you need it.

Use it when you're feeling down.

Use it when you're feeling scared.

Use it when you're feeling like you can't communicate the way you want.

I know... I PROMISE it will make your life better.

I read and listen to affirmations every day, and WOW, have they helped me be the best version of myself! And I want that for you too, my new friends.

Excited? Let's go!

Chapter 1

Affirmations for Unstoppable Confidence

I am confident.

I am unstoppable.

I am positive.

I believe in myself.

I am cool.

I am calm.

I am unruffled.

I am put together.

I am unfazed.

I am nonchalant.

I am at ease.

Nothing can shake me.

I am hopeful.

I am optimistic.

I am certain.

I have no doubts.

My belief is unshakeable.

I am secure in myself.

I am confident in my abilities.

I am not easily persuaded.

I am assured of my choices.

I choose to move with confidence.

My foundation is solid. I am a rock.

I am not easily moved by the wind.

I will stay positive and move forward.

I will be calm like a stream.

I have confidence in myself.

I will not be ruffled by outside forces.

I am cool and collected at all times.

I will be level-headed for the tasks ahead.

I am sure of myself.

I am sure of my actions.

I move with grace and confidence.

I will be strong today.

I will be mentally smart today.

I am the best version of myself.

I will always move with intention.

I stand steadfast in the river.

I move confidently.

Others are secure with me.

My friends see me as stable and confident.

I am collected and confident in my life.

I will continue to progress forward.

I will choose to be the best me today.

I am the one they follow.

I choose to be optimistic today.

I am better than I was yesterday.

I cannot be persuaded easily.

I do not doubt my abilities.

I am true to myself.

Chapter 2

Affirmations for Endless Motivation

I am persistent with all that I do.

My enthusiasm has no limit.

I have a continuous drive for my goals.

I have an unwavering commitment to pursuing my goals.

I overcome challenges easily.

I stay focused daily.

My determination does not wane.

My passion remains strong over time.

I have great goals.

I conquer my goals with different strategies.

I find inspiration in all my pursuits.

My ambition does not waver.

I take action for my goals.

I motivate myself for academic success.

Resilience is my motivation.

My goals are attainable.

I have purpose and direction.

My drive is infectious.

My motivation ignites others' motivation.

I inspire myself.

I have endless motivation.

I propel positive thoughts.

My positive thoughts are prompt.

I provoke endless success.

I have a spark daily.

I have a positive fire in me daily.

My goals are clear.

My thoughts are concrete.

I affirm greatness for myself.

I remain enthusiastic.

I celebrate big and small achievements for motivation.

My curiosity can motivate me.

My creativity and imagination assist in my motivation.

Perseverance runs through my veins.

Motivation courses through me.

Great family support motivates me.

My challenges don't deter me.

My motivation is top-tier.

I affirm greatness for myself.

I am a better version of myself daily.

Continuous inspiration gets the job done.

Infinite ways to drive myself.

I influence myself to be limitless.

Unending movement leads to my success.

I won't stop motivating my peers.

I motivate others with a positive attitude.

Quitting is not an option.

Endless motivation is non-negotiable.

Confirmation is my motivation.

My motivation is never-ending.

Chapter 3

Affirmations for Unshakable Self-Esteem

I am enough.

I am more than enough.

I can do this.

Today, I am the best me.

I will be the best me today and tomorrow.

No obstacle in my way can stop me.

I have high self-respect.

I have dignity in myself.

My morale is high and mighty.

My confidence speaks for itself.

I hold myself in high self-regard.

I walk with pride in myself.

I move with pride in my stride.

I make positive decisions.

I will not accept less for myself.

My pride shines like the sun.

My morale keeps my friends close.

My friends see my self-respect.

My family is proud of my self-assurance.

I assure my friends to push through.

I will push through.

No burden or obstacle will stop me today.

I do not lack of self-confidence.

I will be unstoppable.

There is no burden placed upon me to slow my stride.

My self-worth will not be minimized.

My ego is optimistic and confident.

I take my actions with gratitude.

I am proud of who I am.

I am proud of who I will become.

My family feels prideful when they see me.

My friends can follow me without issue.

I will move strong an ox.

My mind is clear as a river.

I take delight in every step I choose.

I am sufficient in myself.

I take every day with my head held high.

I am positive about my choices and wants.

I can meet my needs by myself.

I remain strong for my friends.

I remain strong for my family.

I take pleasure in having unshakable self-esteem.

I move with dignity

My friends have faith in me

My family has faith in me and my decisions

I am confident in my abilities and movements

I behave with honor and dignity.

I am confident in my own worth.

I am confident in my own ability to progress.

I am confident in my choices and passions.

Chapter 4

Affirmations for Growing Leadership Skills

I will help others grow and succeed.

I lead with kindness and compassion.

I am a natural leader.

I am becoming a better leader.

I dare to take charge.

My ideas are valuable, and I share them with others.

I am a problem solver.

I inspire others with my positive attitude and actions.

I am a good listener.

I respect the opinions of those around me.

I am responsible for my actions.

I lead by example.

I believe in my ability to make a positive impact.

I am open to learning and growing.

Challenges are opportunities for me to showcase my leadership skills.

I use my voice to speak up for what is right and fair.

I am a team player.

I am confident in expressing my thoughts and ideas.

I am patient and understanding.

I see potential in myself and others.

I embrace challenges.

I am a leader who supports the success of others.

I lead with empathy.

I am a positive role model for my peers.

I create a path for others to follow.

I make wise choices.

I celebrate the strengths of those around me.

I am grateful to lead and learn.

I believe in the power of collaboration.

I trust in my ability to handle any situation with grace and poise.

I foster a sense of belonging to my peers.

I am not afraid to take risks.

I am a leader who communicates effectively.

I am a positive influence on those around me.

I am a leader who values honesty.

I am a leader who values integrity.

I have the strength to stand up for what is right.

I inspire others to be their best selves.

I am a problem solver.

I approach challenges with a can-do attitude.

I am a leader who encourages innovation.

I believe in my ability to lead.

I work hard to achieve my goals.

I appreciate the uniqueness of every individual.

I am a leader who values others.

I am a leader who inspires others to pursue their passions.

I radiate positivity.

I am a responsible leader who takes care of myself and others.

I am resilient.

I will bounce back from any setback.

Chapter 5

Affirmations for a Fun and Playful Day

Today will be a great day of fun.

I will have fun today.

I will use every day as a playful day.

I can turn anything into something fun.

Today is a great day to be whimsical.

Cheerfulness leads to a playful day.

I am comical at the right time.

My lightheartedness is a blessing.

I am high-spirited.

The ability to bring joy leads to creativity.

Imagination leads to creativity.

Today is filled with laughter and joy.

I am open to the moments that come my way.

My day is vibrant and playful.

I invite fun and laughter into my day.

I release any worries.

I am a magnet for playful experiences.

Today, I choose to have a playful mindset.

I radiate positive energy.

Playfulness is my natural state.

I am bringing smiles to those around me.

The more I play, the more joy I attract into my life.

I let go of seriousness.

Today, I choose to dance through challenges.

I am a playful spirit.

Laughter is the sound I choose today.

I approach my tasks with a playful attitude.

I am a playful adventurer.

I find delight in the simple pleasures of life.

I bring a sense of playfulness to every interaction.

Playfulness is the key to unlocking creativity.

I create space for laughter and play.

My heart is light.

I choose to see the world through the lens of play.

I see the opportunity to play and have fun.

Playfulness is my superpower.

I attract fun effortlessly.

I invite in the carefree energy of playfulness.

I find joy in the present moment.

I choose to play with the flow of life.

Playfulness is a gift I give to myself.

I share my playful energy with the world.

I welcome the day with open arms.

I am a creator of joy.

I choose to see challenges as playful puzzles to solve.

I am a guide for lighthearted experiences.

Tasha Tinsley

Playfulness is my secret ingredient.

I attract joy with every step.

I infuse my day with moments of playfulness.

My carefree energy of playfulness guides me.

Chapter 6

Affirmations for Believing in Myself

I am confident in my abilities.

I am worthy of success.

I am capable of achieving my goals.

I believe in my ultimate success.

I empower myself.

I am deserving of success.

I have unwavering faith in what I can accomplish.

Confidence flows through me.

I trust in myself to make the right decisions.

I believe in myself.

I attract success into my life.

I face challenges with resilience.

I am the architect of my destiny.

I am becoming a better version of myself daily.

I trust my intuition.

I am on the right path.

I am a capable and competent individual.

I will open doors to unlimited possibilities.

I am surrounded by positivity.

I believe in my own worth.

I am a unique and valuable person.

I know I have the skills to succeed.

I am turning my dreams into reality.

I trust in my ability to learn, adapt, and overcome.

I am inspiring others to believe in themselves.

Believing in myself is the key to unlocking my full potential.

I am capable.

I am strong.

I am resilient.

Confidence is my second nature.

I believe in my dreams.

I face challenges with courage.

My confidence grows stronger with each passing day.

I trust in my journey.

I am deserving of all the good things that life has to offer.

I believe in myself.

I trust in my strengths to guide me through any situation.

I believe in my potential to make a positive impact on the world.

I trust in my ability to achieve my goals.

I have complete faith in myself.

I nurture myself and my mind every day.

I believe in my power to create change.

I am capable of so much positivity.

I trust in my journey.

Confidence flows through me.

I radiate confidence in all that I do.

I will achieve greatness in my life.

I inspire others to trust in their potential.

I am destined for success.

I believe in myself and my progress.

Chapter 7

Affirmations for Embracing My Uniqueness

I celebrate my individuality.

My authentic self is a powerful expression of self-love and acceptance.

I am a one-of-a-kind creation.

My uniqueness is my strength.

I embrace the beauty of my differences.

I am comfortable in my skin.

I inspire others to embrace their uniqueness.

My uniqueness is a gift.

I am proud of the person I am becoming.

I choose to be true to myself.

I honor the quirks that make 'me' me.

My uniqueness is a beacon of light.

I am not meant to fit in; I am meant to stand out.

I embrace my uniqueness.

I accept the essence of who I am.

I celebrate the diversity within me.

My individuality is a source of power.

I am proud of my identity.

I stand tall in my authenticity.

Embracing my individuality gives me strength.

I am a rare and valuable gem.

I shine and rise in my way.

I proudly showcase my identity to the world.

Societal expectations do not define me.

I define myself through authenticity.

I am an original.

I contribute my special gifts with pride.

I am a trailblazer.

My uniqueness is a treasure.

I am a work of art in progress.

I embrace the journey of self-discovery.

My individuality is my greatest asset.

I am comfortable being me.

I am a symphony of talents.

My uniqueness is a source of inspiration for me.

I choose self-acceptance over self-judgment.

I am a rare combination of strengths.

I stand out in a crowd.

I am not afraid to be different.

I celebrate the diversity within me.

I am an original creation.

My uniqueness is my signature.

I sign each day with pride and confidence.

I celebrate the details of my experiences.

I am a masterpiece of originality.

The acceptance of my uniqueness liberates me.

My uniqueness is my power.

I am comfortable in my own skin.

I am an original edition.

I am unique, and it makes me beautiful.

Chapter 8

Affirmations for Kindness and Friendship

I radiate kindness.

My heart is open.

I am a beacon of warmth and compassion.

I create a ripple effect of friendship around me.

I am surrounded by people who appreciate and reciprocate my kindness.

My kindness is a gift.

I effortlessly connect with others through kindness.

My friendships flourish.

I am a magnet for kind-hearted individuals.

Today, I chose kindness.

My circle of friends is a reflection of my kindness.

I embrace the joy of giving.

I am a friend who listens with empathy.

I am a safe space for my friends.

My life is filled with loyal friends.

I am grateful for the kind-hearted friends in my life.

My actions radiate genuine friendship and kindness.

My actions radiate kindness.

I am a source of positivity.

My kindness is the foundation of my friendships.

I am a true friend.

I support and uplift those around me.

I attract friends who appreciate my sincerity.

My kindness is a powerful force.

I have friends who inspire and uplift me with their kindness.

My heart is a wellspring of kindness.

I nurture my friendships with acts of kindness.

I am surrounded by friends.

I take joy in making acts of kindness.

My friendships are a display of my kindness.

I show patience and care.

I show goodwill towards my friends.

I have compassion for the world.

I am generous with my kindness.

I have decency for the feelings of others.

I will show concern for others in tough times.

I will have a gentleness for others.

I show affection to my friends and family.

I have a warmth in my heart.

My selflessness allows me to help others.

I have goodwill with my community.

The generosity I show others is a reflection of my person.

I will act with benevolence today.

I will act with compassion and sympathy.

I show concern and tenderness for others in struggle.

Today, I will be humane towards others.

I will show compassion for my fellow friends.

I am kind.

I am a great friend.

My affection towards others is a show of my kindness.

Chapter 9

Affirmations for Being a Great Leader

I am a pioneer.

I am a pacesetter.

I will take the lead.

I will set the example.

I will set the trend.

I am a trendsetter.

I am an innovator.

Others follow the pace I set.

There is no imitator against me.

I will lead my followers and friends in the right direction.

I can direct my friends in the right direction.

I am the head of my ship.

I am the captain of my destiny.

People look up to me for directions.

I will lead with dignity and grace.

I take pride in my movement forward.

I will lead with safety and kindness.

I will lead with care and trust.

I will let others know what to do to progress forward.

I am in control of myself.

I am in control of my own destiny.

I am a visionary.

I am inspirational to others.

I am empathetic to my whims and goals.

I will be an effective communicator.

I will be resilient to the detours of the world.

I will be decisive in my leadership.

I will mentor others for greatness.

I will mentor with positivity.

I will be better.

I will be a great leader.

I will be accountable.

I will hold others accountable and lead in the right direction.

I will lead with integrity.

I will lead with honesty.

I will lead with character.

My inner compass is a guide for others.

My inner morals guide my thoughts and actions.

I am driven by my mission of success.

I will be dedicated to my cause.

I will be understanding of my peers.

I will be empathetic to my peers.

I will make the right decisions.

The pressures of the world will not bind me.

I will be trustworthy.

I will empower others every day.

I will communicate clearly.

I will be resilient.

I will be strong.

I will be a good leader today.

Chapter 10

Affirmations for Exploring the World

I am an adventurous spirit.

Every journey I embark upon opens my mind.

I embrace the unknown.

I am ready to discover the world's hidden treasures.

I find joy in the excitement of exploration.

I appreciate the beauty of our world.

Traveling expands my horizons.

I welcome the fun of exploration.

I enjoy each destination I visit.

I am open to the magic that comes with exploring new places.

The world is full of awe-inspiring landscapes.

My curiosity knows no bounds.

I savor the flavors of different foods.

Exploring the world allows me to connect with others.

I am a fearless explorer.

I am constantly seeking new adventures and discoveries.

I appreciate the story of each place I visit.

Exploring ignites my creativity.

I am always ready for the next adventure.

I am grateful to explore the world and create lasting memories.

The more I explore, the more I realize the beauty of humanity.

I seek out hidden gems and off-the-beaten-path destinations.

I look forward to all the fun in my exploration.

Exploring the world is truly a gift.

I cherish the friendships forged through my travels.

Each journey let me delve into the beauty of the world.

I carry the things I learned from my travels.

The world is my classroom, and I am a student.

I find joy in my travels.

I enjoy traveling the world.

I am exploring the world every day.

I will find a new adventure today.

I am excited to delve into new places.

I will examine all around me.

I will search for a new adventure.

A new adventure will find me today.

I will tour the world.

I will traverse all that I can see.

I will investigate my surroundings.

I will always seek the next adventure.

I enjoy the traveling that I get to do daily.

I will leave no stone unturned.

I will make sure to survey my surroundings.

I will take the lead in exploring my home.

I love learning new things.

I will keep an open mind.

I will take the time to learn new things.

I will not neglect a new adventure.

I will not overlook a new area.

I will be a great explorer.

Chapter 11

Affirmations for Learning and Growing Every Day

I will continue to learn every day.

Every day, I grow stronger.

Daily, I grow smarter.

I am a creative thinker.

I will study to get better.

I approach challenges with optimism and a can-do attitude.

I will train hard to become better.

I will continue my learning.

I am developing into a better person.

I will continue to flourish.

I will continue to spread my love.

Every day, I will get better.

I am a curious learner.

Mistakes are a natural part of learning.

I am a resilient learner.

Each lesson I learn is a building block.

I love learning.

I am open-minded.

I am growing more and more patient.

I am capable of finding unique solutions to any problem.

I understand that progress takes time.

I celebrate my achievements.

I believe in my ability to grasp new concepts.

I enjoy the process of learning.

I am a lifelong learner.

I use my imagination daily.

I am excited about my path ahead.

I am not afraid to ask questions.

I believe in my capacity to learn.

I am surrounded by opportunities for learning.

I am a creative problem solver.

I am persistent in my learning.

I am a sponge for knowledge.

I celebrate the continuous growth in my abilities.

Learning is a lifelong adventure.

I am a responsible learner.

I believe in my potential.

I learn from my experiences.

I am a valuable learner.

My skills and knowledge are constantly evolving.

I am open to trying new things.

I am a proactive learner.

I am a positive learner.

I am a team player.

I am a mindful learner.

I am a responsible learner.

I am a motivated learner.

I am a balanced learner.

I am a grateful learner.

I am a shining learner.

Chapter 12

Affirmations for Building Strong Relationships

I am a good friend, and I attract good friends into my life.

I treat others with kindness and respect, and they treat me the same way.

My words have power in any relationship.

I am patient and understanding.

I choose friends who bring out the best in me.

Every day, I learn and grow in my ability to connect with others.

I am open-minded and appreciate the unique qualities of my friends.

I communicate my feelings honestly and respectfully with my friends.

I show people in my life love and appreciation.

My heart is open to kindness.

I listen with my ears.

I am patient and understanding and accept my friends' differences.

Every day, I become better at making friends.

I choose friends who make me feel happy and supported.

I am a positive influence on my friends.

My friends bring positivity into my life.

I use my words to build others up and express my feelings respectfully.

I am a good team player and enjoy cooperating with others.

My friendships are based on trust, honesty, and mutual respect.

I celebrate the success and achievements of my friends.

I am grateful for the special people in my life.

I am brave enough to apologize and forgive when needed.

I am a good communicator.

I make a difference by being a good friend to others.

I am surrounded by love and support from my friends and family.

I learn and grow through my relationships with others.

I am surrounded by people who appreciate and value me.

I attract friends who inspire me to be me.

I am kind, loving, and understanding in my relationships.

I create harmony and joy in my friendships.

I choose friends who lift me.

I am a good listener, and my friends feel heard and understood.

I am excited to meet new friends.

I am confident in my ability to build and maintain positive relationships.

My words uplift and encourage my friends.

My friends encourage me to reach my goals

Communication is needed in every relationship.

I maintain contact with everyone in my relationships.

I link with people with a great mindset.

I can bond with people with similar goals to mine.

My network is full of greatness.

I use my network to reach success.

My network wants to see me grow.

My peers value themselves and me.

I can be a healthy individual in my relationships.

I won't lie to build relationships.

I am a good listener.

Compassion can be built into relationships.

I give myself and my friends grace.

Patience in relationships provides longevity.

Chapter 13

Affirmations for Achieving Big Dreams

I am capable of turning my dreams into reality.

Each day, I take steps towards my big dreams.

My dreams are within reach.

Challenges provide me with opportunities to grow and achieve my goals.

I am committed to my vision.

My dreams are like stars guiding me through the darkest nights.

Every small effort I make is a building block towards my big dreams.

I trust in my abilities.

I am the architect of my destiny.

With passion and purpose, I turn my dreams into tangible achievements.

My dreams fuel my actions.

I am resilient.

I attract positive opportunities that align with my dreams and goals.

I am a magnet for success.

My dreams are the blueprint for success.

I persevere in the face of obstacles.

I deserve to achieve my dreams.

It is okay to applaud myself.

I'll celebrate every step forward, acknowledging my progress.

My belief in myself is unwavering.

I possess the courage to pursue my dreams.

I am a powerhouse.

My dreams are like seeds; with patience, they blossom into reality.

I am surrounded by the energy of success.

I am the author of my story.

My dreams are my compass.

I am worthy of achieving big dreams.

Challenges are temporary.

My dreams are permanent.

I attract solutions and opportunities that align with my dreams.

Each day, I am closer to my most ambitious dreams.

My mind is a powerhouse of creative ideas to manifest my dreams.

I am committed to lifelong learning.

I constantly enhance my skills to achieve my dreams.

My dreams inspire me to push beyond my comfort zone.

I am unstoppable.

My dreams are inevitable.

It is okay to be proud of myself.

I write my determination and purpose.

I welcome the opportunities that come my way.

I am grateful for the journey towards my dreams.

I am determined.

My dreams lead me to my true destination.

I embrace my journey.

I align my dreams.

My dreams lead me to new heights of achievement.

I am persistent.

Growth leads to my dreams.

My dreams are worthy.

I have a vision for my destiny.

Chapter 14

Affirmations for Positive Self-Talk

I am smart.

I have unique talents that make me special.

I am kind.

I am loved.

I am creative.

I am strong and capable.

I am responsible.

I am a good friend.

I am brave.

I am a good listener.

I am patient.

I am honest.

I am a problem solver.

I am respectful.

I am joyful.

I am curious.

I am responsible for my actions.

I am unique.

I am grateful for the love in my life.

I am helpful.

I am a good sport.

I am honest about my feelings.

I am a good communicator.

I show kindness to my brothers and sisters.

I am proud of my accomplishments.

I am organized.

I love learning new things.

I am a good student.

I learn from my mistakes.

I am a good person.

I am grateful.

I can share my thoughts clearly.

I am a good teammate.

I am thoughtful.

I collaborate well with others.

I am determined.

I am a good leader.

I can adjust to new situations.

I am confident.

I can achieve my goals with hard work.

I make good choices.

I believe in myself.

I am a good friend who supports my peers.

I am resilient.

I am generous.

I care for the environment.

I am a good communicator.

I enjoy assisting others.

I am a good listener who values the opinions of others.

I am a cheerful and capable individual.

Chapter 15

Affirmations for Spreading Joy and Positivity

I am unique and special just the way I am.

I believe in myself and my abilities.

My imagination is incredible!

I love myself.

I am filled with joy.

I spread positivity.

I spread joy.

I am a thrill to be around.

I take enjoyment in spreading joy.

I am capable of achieving anything I set my mind to.

My actions make a difference.

I have the power to make a positive impact on the world around me.

I am a kind and caring person.

I am loved and valued by those around me.

I have a great imagination.

I am filled with glee!

I am making a positive difference in my life.

My friendships bring joy to my life.

I am surrounded by love.

I love learning new things every day.

I can handle my responsibilities with care.

I value what others have to say.

I am patient and know that good things take time.

I am honest, and I choose to tell the truth.

I find creative solutions to challenges.

I treat others the way I want to be treated.

I find happiness in the little things.

I explore the world around me with wonder.

I learn from my mistakes with delight.

I will continually spread joy to my family.

I am grateful for the love and support in my life.

I enjoy assisting others.

I enjoy making others happy.

I am proud of myself.

I keep my belongings in order.

I enjoy my own well-being.

I am a good kid.

I learn from different perspectives.

I am a good friend.

I am grateful for my talents and abilities.

I enjoy bringing bliss to my family and friends.

I enjoy the positivity of others.

I will continually spread a feeling of pleasure.

The joy I have is boundless.

I will keep spreading positivity in the world.

I will not despair.

I will push forward with my joy.

I take pleasure in seeing others happy.

I am so happy today!

I choose to remain happy today!

Chapter 16

Affirmations for Overcoming Challenges

I am capable of achieving anything I set my mind to.

I express myself openly.

I am strong and resilient; I can overcome any challenge.

Challenges help me grow.

I dare to face difficult situations with confidence.

Every challenge is an opportunity for me to learn and improve.

I am open to asking for help when I need it.

I believe in my ability to find solutions.

I am determined.

I trust in my abilities to tackle challenges head-on.

I won't give up when faced with challenges.

I approach challenges with a positive attitude.

I am resourceful and creative.

I focus on what I can control and let go of what I cannot.

I break down challenges into smaller tasks.

I am a problem solver.

I learn from every challenge.

I can find solutions to any challenge.

I know that progress is a journey.

I bounce back stronger after facing challenges.

Challenges are opportunities for me to showcase my strengths.

I approach challenges with patience.

I am encouraged by challenges.

I have a positive mindset that helps me navigate through challenges.

I trust the process of growth and development.

I am patient with myself.

I am not alone.

I can seek support from those who care about me.

I am a problem-solving superstar.

I find strength in adversity.

I approach challenges with a focused mind.

I am adaptable.

I am tough.

I am motivated to overcome them and succeed.

Challenges are my puzzles to solve.

I am a warrior.

I have the strength to face challenges.

I trust myself to handle whatever comes my way.

Challenges are stepping stones to my greatness.

I am not afraid of challenges.

I face challenges with a positive mindset.

I am a problem-solving genius.

Challenges are just part of my winning journey.

I am a champion.

I am a quick learner.

I face challenges with a smile.

I trust myself to find solutions.

I am a conqueror.

I am capable and strong.

I can overcome any challenge.

Chapter 17

Affirmations for Being Brave and Resilient

I can bounce back from challenges.

I express myself safely.

I am brave.

I choose to be brave.

I face challenges with courage.

I am strong.

Today, I choose to be courageous.

I can overcome any obstacle.

I am a warrior.

Being brave allows me to step with confidence.

I am resilient!

Bravery is a choice.

I am not defined by fear.

I face challenges head-on.

I am courageous.

I am brave in my pursuits.

I am bold.

I am brave enough to express my true self.

Each day, I grow more confident.

I am a beacon of courage.

Bravery is within me.

I am not afraid to take risks.

I am ready for whatever comes my way.

I stand firm when faced with the unknown.

I welcome challenges.

I can overcome all obstacles.

I trust myself.

Each step I take is a bold one.

I am fearless.

I am heroic.

I am gallant.

I am a brave adventurer.

I choose to move with courage today.

I am not limited by fear.

I am bold and daring today.

I am determined to go forward.

I trust myself to face difficulties.

I am lionhearted.

Bravery is my foundation.

I am unafraid of the path ahead.

I am propelled forward by bravery.

I am ready to be called upon when needed.

My spirit is indomitable.

I am resolute in my choices and decisions.

My past fears do not define me.

I am gutsy.

I am ballsy.

I am brave in moments of uncertainty.

I am not fearful of today's outcomes.

I embrace the unknown.

Chapter 18

Affirmations for Creative Adventures

I am a creative explorer.

I will let my imagination soar.

My ideas are magical seeds.

I create a world only I can imagine.

I am a brave artist.

My creativity knows no bounds.

My creativity has endless possibilities.

I am a storyteller with my creativity.

The more I create, the more my imagination expands.

I will dream big and create even bigger.

I am a shining star in my creative galaxy.

My ideas fit together perfectly.

There are no limits or rules.

I paint with laughter and sprinkle my stories with joy.

Each art project is a unique expression of my awesome self.

I am an inventor of the world.

My imagination is a treasure chest full of endless wonders.

My ideas and thoughts dance.

I orchestrate my creativity.

Every mistake is a chance to discover something new.

I am an architect of dreams, building castles in my mind.

My creativity blooms.

I'm innovative.

I create magic.

I sail the seas of my imagination.

My ideas are like fireworks.

I am a creator.

I will sculpt my thoughts for flow.

I am a masterpiece.

I write with fury.

My creativity is a superpower.

I'm a visionary.

I have a solid imagination.

I'm the original.

I am an artist.

I will turn ordinary moments into extraordinary adventures.

My mind is a playground where creativity flows.

I'm prolific.

I love adventure.

I mold my creativity and happiness together.

My ideas flow.

My creativity is a treasure.

I am a master storyteller.

I shape the world of my dreams.

Today, I will let my creativity sparkle and shine.

I am a wizard of creativity.

My imagination is a beautiful pattern of ideas.

I'm gifted and creative.

My imagination runs deep.

My creativity leads me to new experiences.

Chapter 19

Affirmations for Loving My Family

I love my family.

My family and I grow stronger daily.

I am thankful for my family.

My family builds me up.

My family and I build together.

My family and I support each other.

Family members are not enemies.

My family and I will have wealth.

As a family, we stand united.

Our family understands respect.

My family respects each other.

Family is affectionate.

Family is amiable.

Family is caring.

Our clan is attentive.

We are a devoted household.

Family can be generous.

Our kin is giant on TLC.

Tender, loving care builds a family.

My family makes me proud.

Our home is peaceful and safe.

My family keeps us safe.

My family keeps me safe.

Communication works well in my family.

My parents connect with me.

My parents guide me.

Quality time with my family is the best.

My family is encouraging.

I have a strong support system.

My family teaches me kindness.

My family accepts me.

My family gave me good coping skills.

I am honest with my family.

I am honest with my parents.

Family means everything to me.

My family keeps me calm.

The love of my family is a source of peace.

I am a loving and supportive member of my family.

My love positively influences my family.

I am surrounded by the love of my family.

I am grateful for my family.

My family is a sanctuary.

I am committed to my family.

The love in my family is powerful.

My family is strong.

My family has pride.

My family makes me proud to be one of them.

The most important thing is family.

My family is my home.

I am grateful for my family and their guidance.

Chapter 20

Affirmations for a Bright and Happy Future

My future is as bright as the sun in the sky.

Every day brings me closer to a world of joy and wonder.

My future is full of colorful possibilities.

I'm destined for greatness.

The world is full of exciting adventures.

My future is filled with dreams.

I am like a kite soaring high.

I am a tiny seed growing into a mighty tree.

I am a superhero in the making.

My future is my superhero story.

Tasha Tinsley

I am a little explorer.

I am a shining star.

My future is beautiful and transformative.

I am a bubble of joy.

I am the wizard of my own destiny.

I am a happy seed planted in the garden.

I am like a rainbow after the rain.

My future is bright.

I am a little fish with big dreams.

My future is filled with happiness.

My future will bloom with success.

I will continue to make others smile.

I am little now, but I have big dreams.

I am a tiny acorn growing into a mighty oak.

The world will be better because I'm in it.

I am a beam of sunlight.

I am a little architect of my future.

I am discovering new wonders for my future.

My future is going to be full of possibilities.

I will do my best.

My dreams are worthwhile.

The future is full of happiness.

I may be young, but my choices matter.

I am a star.

I am a happy camper.

I am young, and my words are powerful.

My future is boundless.

I will make a difference in the world.

The future is unpredictable, but I am ready and capable.

I am sailing towards my bright future.

My actions are powerful and have meaning.

My future is full of successes.

My future is bright.

I will stay positive and bold.

My tomorrow will be the brightest.

I am excited to see what my future holds.

I am ready and eager to see what the future holds.

I am the future.

I shine the brightest.

My future is the brightest.